QUARRELS

Quarrels

Eve Joseph

PROSE POEMS

anvil press • vancouver

Anvil Press Publishers Inc.
P.O. Box 3008, Main Post Office
Vancouver, B.C. V6B 3X5 Canada
www.anvilpress.com

Library and Archives Canada Cataloguing in Publication

Joseph, Eve, 1953-, author
Quarrels / Eve Joseph. — First edition.

Poems.
ISBN 978-1-77214-119-1 (softcover)

I. Title.

PS8619.O84Q37 2018   C811'.6   C2018-901892-5

Printed and bound in Canada
Cover design by Marijke Friesen
Interior by HeimatHouse
Author photo: Sandy Powlik
Represented in Canada by Publishers Group Canada
Distributed by Raincoast Books

The publisher gratefully acknowledges the financial assistance of the Canada
Council for the Arts, the Canada Book Fund, and the Province of British
Columbia through the B.C. Arts Council and the Book Publishing Tax Credit.

For Jonah, Ava and Jake

Table of Contents

Part Two

Part Three

We make out of the quarrel with others, rhetoric,
but of the quarrel with ourselves, poetry.
— W.B. Yeats

PART ONE

…a little later, she discovered
the goal of art was not the truth but the
marvelous — indeed, the marvelous was the truth.
— Joan Acocella

THE TRAIN BLEW THROUGH THE STATION WITHOUT braking. On the platform, babies lifted out of their carriages and dropped back down into the arms of strangers. Nobody could figure out who belonged to whom. It was a lottery of mothers and fathers, lonely aunts and childless couples. A man who looked just like me scooped me up and together we went home to meet my mother who was working on a jigsaw puzzle at the kitchen table. I fit right into place but my father didn't. He was not blue like the sky or grey like the arched bridge. The station was littered with hats. I set up a booth and sold them for a slight profit. My father glowed with pride.

NOW THAT I LIVE BY THE SEA, I AM NEVER SURE WHAT THE day will bring. Gulls stomp on the roof like heavy-footed prowlers causing me to wake in alarm. Broken shells litter the garden: clam, oyster and torn crab pincers serrated like nutcrackers. I'm standing at the window, sipping my morning coffee, when I see her. My mother is rowing against the current in the rain. I cup my hands and yell, *Come in for a gin and tonic*. It's not that awful rowing toward God, nothing that dramatic. It's just her, after all these years, the creak of oarlocks and a small wake trailing behind. Like the hapless Aeschylus I walk bareheaded, forgetting to look up at what might be hurtling toward me.

THE CAPON EXPLODED OUT OF THE PRESSURE COOKER AND stuck in the kitchen ceiling. It hung there like a black chandelier. People took turns trying to pull it out with no success. Its charred head poked out of the roof and acted as a weather vane. The wind polished it until it gleamed like a well-worn doorknob. We adjusted to the smell of burnt bones and set the table as usual. In the 9th century, Pope Nicholas decreed that a cock had to top every church steeple in Europe. Our home was a holy place. We worshipped all that crawled. All that flew.

WE MET AT A BIRTHDAY PARTY. YOU WERE THE ONLY RUM drinker in the room. On the couch, Al Purdy was going on about the stunted trees in the Arctic. Upon closer examination, we could see that the leaves were tiny parkas. The illogical must have a logic of its own you said. The first two drinks don't count, it's the third that blows the door open. With every gust of wind the little coats raised their arms and waved shyly at us. You were a new music, something I had not heard before. As they used to say about that Estonian composer: he only had to shake his sleeves and the notes would fall out.

THE RAIN HAS STOPPED AND THE SKY HAS CLEARED. MY husband is downstairs chatting with Milosz, who is chopping vegetables for dinner. I can't make out the words, only the swell of the sea and those two soldiers rowing. Milosz is wearing my apron and drinking my wine. The tide has come in, erasing the muddy footprints and the sign for *Help* carved in the sand. How do we ever return? How is it possible? I'm told a massive tree flourishes in the heart of the favela, like the pink lungs of a coal miner. He puts the oar down and caresses me with his calloused hands. He knows who he is. Not the cook; the other one.

I RARELY LEAVE MY ROOM BY THE SEA. WHEN I GO OUT, THE fish vendor smiles at me and the woman stirring fudge in the beaten copper pot nods. Every day the chambermaid changes my sheets and leaves new bars of lavender soap in the little basket. Afraid to return to my old life, I want to live like Max Jacob — in comfort at the Hotel Nollet, entertaining writers, painters and the occasional shy novice. Crouching down, I can see my past life through the keyhole. There were weddings and funerals in the village every weekend. Each closet had at least one black dress.

YOU ARE FLOATING ON YOUR BACK IN THE SALT WATER. A little cork bobbing in the waves. A moment of infinity, brief but intense. Or, you are trying to imagine yourself as an old woman getting on a bus in Aarhus and feeling beautiful for no particular reason. Or, you are searching for a Danish poet only to find, when you look him up, that he is a pathologist. You think poets and pathologists probably have a great deal in common. Engaged, as they both are, in the peculiar and the wonder-like. Which in the Danish — *underligt* — means exactly the same thing.

WHERE HAVE ALL THE STUTTERERS GONE? DEMOSTHENES shouting at the sea with pebbles in his mouth, for example. And Newton, who asked himself why, without gravity, birds can't sing. Jim Darby, turning scarlet at the front of the class, opening and closing his mouth like a fish. It's 1961. The teacher is holding a fly rod. He's casting it toward Jim. Patiently reeling it in and casting again. Hooking the words and drawing them out one at a time. We feel them caught at the back of our own throats. Little shits, some of us are laughing. The tackle box is full of shiny lures and brilliant feathers. There is in no hurry. Like any fisherman, he has all the time in the world.

STRANGER TO HERSELF, SHE IS THE ONE THE OTHER recognizes. A face in the rain-streaked window of a passing bus. A hand pointing the way to the widow's cottage. Fields, broken fences, the steady tinnitus of insects on an August evening. In her ninety-first year, rocking on the porch, she watches Rilke's birds flying soundlessly between *soul and sky*. There is no place that does not see her. The nightly exodus of crows begins. Wave after wave of those elegant clerics on their way to god-knows-where. A place they can plan some kind of banditry, a hole-in-the-wall for those with a price on their heads.

MY MOTHER WAS A WHITE SHEET DRYING ON THE LINE. Wooden clothespins held her tight as she lifted and snapped and filled like a sail. At night, when she covered me, I inhaled lily of the valley, burning leaves, the starched collar of a nurse's uniform and the stillness of a recently abandoned room. She taught me how to iron the creases out of a man's shirt after all the men had disappeared. My mother played piano by ear in the basement. A long line of hungry people gathered outside to hear her play. They wanted news from home. Overhead, handkerchiefs fluttered in the breeze. Little telegrams sent but never delivered.

FROGS FELL FROM THE SKY AND LANDED ON THE ROOF OF the Citroën. Caught in the headlights, they bounced like gymnasts on the road in front of us. A plague? A child's game? We'd hitchhiked a long way from home. Meteors shot across the heavens. *Each one's a death*, said the girl in the backseat. No, I countered, *each one's a wish*. The trick is to return to the moment. To smell the butts in the ashtray, the air freshener dangling from the mirror. *Stairway to Heaven* was playing on the radio. God arms himself with his smallest creations. Through the windshield, the amphibians looked like embryos. Little replicas from the illustrated textbook of medical miracles and anomalies.

I WAIT FOR SNOW IN A CITY WHERE IT RAINS FOR WEEKS on end. People walk by the Cathedral in the slush. They don't think about the ten bronze bells hanging motionless in the belfry like late September pears. Children line up in twos in front of the church school, jostling each other on the stairs, establishing their petty hierarchies when they think God is not looking. In his tower, overlooking the YWCA, the bell-ringer imagines he's Quasimodo. Every day the temperature hovers just above zero. There's no point attaching sleigh bells to the pony's harness. There's just no point at all.

LIGHT STUTTERS DOWN THE CLOSED BLINDS AND BUILDS a spine, one vertebrae at a time up the bedroom wall. It lengthens across the hotel room like a man searching the woods with a flashlight for something he has lost: a set of keys, a worn wallet, the dog he let out at dawn to pee. The sighted lead the blind by the hand knowing, at some point, they will let go. Follow the light, the living say to the dying. The logic in that escapes me. I have always been drawn to the shadows. Light arcs across the room and bends at the corner like a hinge. A door that could open but remains closed. The deeper the man goes, the thinner the beam of light until he's lost amongst the blue coffins of trees.

ANOTHER DAY IN PARADISE READ THE SIGN ON THE CAFÉ door. The ocean adzed in sunlight. Soup simmering on the stove. At a corner table, Breton was arguing with Artaud about a fly in the water pitcher. One wanted to fish it out, one wanted to let it drown. *I shit on Marxism*, said the madman to the surrealist. It was Wednesday. A local improv group was about to perform. One of the actors sat down at a white piano in an imaginary asylum. The audience loved the idea of madness but recoiled at language that glistened like a weapon.

SHE BEGAN WITH THE IDEA THAT LITTLE IS KNOWN AND much is troubling. Her father escaped to a place where she couldn't find him. In his new home, nobody knew his stories. He was happy. Isn't that what we want? To address a rapt audience as if for the first time? He sent her love letters with no return address. She rewrote them as sonnets. Confessional poetry didn't interest her. She preferred her memory barracked. Better, she thought, to walk within the confines of the barbed wire fence.

THE DAUGHTER OF A HOLOCAUST SURVIVOR HAD HER
father's number tattooed on her ankle after he died. Unfortu-
nately, she got the number wrong so had it blotted out, and her
father's correct number tattooed below. Later, she discovered that
the wrong number was a real person, a Dutch Jew who died at
age 30 in the camp. Her ankle is turning black. The dots, having
bled into each other, look like forget-me-nots. Little flowers
nobody recognizes anymore. The sad truth about Theodor Adorno
is that he will be remembered for one thing and one thing only.

BECAUSE THEY SAID IT COULDN'T BE DONE, I DID IT. EVERY-one agreed it was impossible. It wasn't hard. The trick was not to think. A man clearing wet leaves from the drains shook his head. A family set aside their differences. In the hospital, a woman who could no longer speak began to sing. It was a small thing, really. I've almost forgotten the details. There was a silo of light. A pair of needle-nosed pliers beside a jar of hooks. Peace was restored. When consulted, the medium said there had never been any doubt. The ghost had come home. It was here to stay.

YOU KNOCK ON THE DOOR BUT NOBODY ANSWERS. CUPPING your hands around your face you peer through the side-panel of frosted glass. A kettle is whistling, a woman singing as she sets the table. This is a familiar house. You knock again. Inside, the sounds are festive. Glasses clink and a band starts up. Pressing your ear to the door, you hear the sound of your own laughter. This is the house you grew up in. You're sure of it now. The revelers are boisterous, their dancing shadows on the lawn. Your legs are cold, there's frost on your shoes, and the cabby calls impatiently from the street. You remember a song that eluded you all day.

THE ANGEL IS AN ARGUMENT AGAINST REASON. HE'S HARD of hearing and when he reaches out his hands they shake and he never knows whose fall he'll break. The one that caught me on a July afternoon — inside the silence of the accident — and cradled me in the middle of the road, was like an uncle I'd never met. One who didn't measure up and was never seen at family gatherings. A bachelor who went to see a holy man in a crowded field and was told by the disciple, *What you want can never be*.

EVERY DAY, FROM THE BALCONY, I WATCH THREE BABY gulls rehearse. One flaps its wings like Otto Lilienthal, the glider king, and runs toward the gutter, teetering on the edge. Another jumps up and down as if gathering courage on the edge of a diving board. A third quotes Nietzsche: *and those who were seen dancing were thought to be insane by those who could not hear the music.* Magi of the rooftops or a triumvirate of fools? Hard to say. There must be a moment to surrender to the updraft. In the gnarled tree down the road a crow, one eye on the performance, is gorging on apples.

COCKROACHES SWARMED OVER THE DECKS. THEY CASCADED out of the cutlery drawer and fell with a click into the stainless steel sink. Each one was an oracle. On calm nights, when the moon was a porthole through which our ship sailed, the pantry hummed with their prophecies. God spoke to us through them. I gave leftover scraps to the workers in port — pickled herring and black bread — and they brought me burlap sacks stuffed with green mangoes. On long voyages, we wore gloves in bed to keep the roaches from gnawing our fingernails.

IN GRADE THREE, MISS GLADSTONE SHOWED US HOW TO press leaves between wax paper with a hot iron. She taught us about photosynthesis and we lifted our spindly arms and swayed like trees. Some of us were maples, some poplars. When the breeze picked up, our crimson leaves twirled on their stems and fell at our feet. Branches held high, we breathed out what the world breathed in. We didn't know this was praise. Our faces, perfectly preserved, decorated the classroom windows. Press down, the late poet said, press down over and over again. This was the lesson. This was what we took away.

WHAT DO SAILORS TALK ABOUT IN THE OLD MARINER'S home on a Tuesday afternoon in Oslo? Their sweaters are worn at the elbows and their hands tremble when they roll their cigarettes. Rough seas, heat, hard work are largely forgotten. One picks bits of tobacco off his lip and tongue. Their thoughts are rheumy, flowing into each other. Of course they are talking about the weather like everybody else. Unlike Cortez, they discovered no new lands, conquered nothing. It's snowing again. The fjords are green and silent. The whalers sit apart from the others; whether out of arrogance or camaraderie it's impossible to say.

MY MOTHER TOOK ME TO A MOTEL TO WATCH THE ECLIPSE. Birds fell silent and the temperature dropped. A line of darkness crossed the continent. She made a pinhole camera out of an empty pack of Camel cigarettes. Scallops, crescents, batman icons climbed the walls. Little moons spilled on the floor and onto our feet. Unsure if the world was ending, she pulled on her white gloves and opened the door to the growing twilight. Through the leaves, the eclipses on the sidewalk looked like scales. Together we walked on the back of a marvelous fish. Somebody was tying a fly at a kitchen table. Someone was about to cast a long line.

ALL SONS GO WHERE THEIR MOTHERS CAN'T FOLLOW. They disappear through secret tunnels behind bookcases and down trap doors with brass rings. Mine escaped through the glow-in-the-dark stars on his ceiling. I thought I saw him once on Aconcagua free-soloing in the Andes amongst the ruby-throated sylphs and thin-winged ghosts. I waved wildly but the border patrol stamped my passport and shoved me along. When the snows came, heavy and silent, the mountain wore a wedding dress with a long scalloped train. How lucky my son is, I thought, to be with that beautiful bride.

THE CARETAKER RESCUES WOMEN FROM THE DEGRADA-tions of the night. He brings them home to his mother, combing her long gray hair. This could be a sordid story but it's not. He lies down with the women, reading the Kabbalah aloud and circling the fiery bits with a red marker. When he's not saving whores, he's sitting in front of a large screen, bathed in blue light. At night, he walks with Rahab through the streets of Jericho. The two of them searching for the rope, the window and the wall. His tiny apartment smells of cat piss, the narrow bed tucked in tightly as a prison bunk. Maybe I'm wrong. This is a sordid story after all.

MY GRANDFATHER LAY MOTIONLESS BENEATH A CHENILLE bedspread. His upturned hands drifting like tiny boats. He was coming and going through the open window, a little further each time. Chestnuts, spiked like medieval maces, lay on the ground in what looked to be the aftermath of a long and arduous battle. *Death is inside the bones,* wrote Neruda, *like a barking where there are no dogs.* I kept my distance. Behind me, my father was on his knees by the hospital bed. I couldn't tell if he was praying. On the wall, his shadow leaned slightly forward. As if wanting to comfort but hesitating to intrude.

THE NAME I WAS GIVEN BELONGS TO ANOTHER WOMAN. At night she reads *The Man Who Stole Dreams* to my children and exchanges the baby teeth they place under their pillows for cash. I am grateful to her at the same time I hate her for being a thief. People I was once close to have no idea where to begin searching. One has been waiting in the pool hall for forty-seven years. He takes my clarinet out of its red velvet case and wets the reed so that it will be supple when I return. The woman is kneeling at a grave with my initials carved on it. On the other side of the wrought iron fence, mossy stones lean like old men who have taken out their hearing aids. *Sit*, they say, *tell us who you are.*

DARKNESS ARRIVES WITHOUT DRAWING ATTENTION TO itself. Porch lights flick on down the block. We're bathed in intimacy, a united front against danger — the bin diver, nasty drunk, vicious dog. The girl who works in the corner grocery store sweeps the floors and puts out mousetraps. A few dry leaves rustle in at the door when she shakes out the rug. Under fluorescent lights, she moves like an actress in a one-woman play. Night is preoccupied with arrivals and departures. The woman keeping vigil at her husband's bedside can't say if it's relief or sorrow she feels when he wakes with a shudder at dawn.

IN GRADE SCHOOL, WE MAPPED THE ROUTES OF NOMADS
and believed there was a place on earth for all. Odysseus hears
the lowing of the cattle winding home. The sheep bleating. I
hear nothing over the roar of the plane's engines. Moving as
one thought across the sky, a herd of dumb beasts names itself:
cirrus, altostratus, cumulonimbus. We commence our descent
through an albino ceiling. Like all migrations, this one starts
with a need and ends in a place with no word for *home*.

I TRY TO FOLLOW YOUR LEAD, CHARLES, ONLY TO END UP with a tiny gold key that opens nothing. What am I supposed to do with winter afternoons that last one hundred years and men who subsist on the scent of flowers alone? In the great hall of poets there is no place to leave a message. Unlike the bits of paper tucked into the Wailing Wall, my prayers float like smog over the congested city. It could have been easy you know. The key slipping into the lock, opening a little door. Together we could have entered the garden. I could have watched over you as you slept and placed a cool hand on your fevered brow.

PEOPLE WHO SUFFER FROM BOANTHROPY BELIEVE THEY are cows. In the morning, when the dew is still on the grass, they head out to graze. The farmer thinks of them as a herd but they see themselves as a congregation. The Jerseys welcome all newcomers with rich buttermilk biscuits while the Holsteins hold tight to their Lutheran roots and minister from their pulpits in the barn. Tired of all things human, these people crawl on all fours like Nebuchadnezzar in the stubbled fields outside of Babylon. A motorist, assuming they are searching for something lost, abandons his car and joins the search. Soon he too is lowing and swishing his tail in the tall grass. As with all recent converts, he is zealous. When the farmer shoos him away from the flowerbeds he charges, head down, baseball cap flying into the water trough.

THE POET KEEPS A JAR OF COMMAS ON HIS DESK. THEY look like the sheared ears of voles and are soft as apricots. Late at night, blindfolded, he loves to take them out and play pin-the-tail on the donkey while his wife and children are fast asleep. He plays his sentences like fish in a stream, tickling for trout with curled fingers. Commas are hearing buds he places deep inside his ears. After sprinkling them liberally, he waits for the first sprouts to unfurl. In summer, on hot, dry days, he strings them on the washing line between the tree in the ear and the shelter built out of longing. Get close enough and you can see the little hairs quivering.

ALL AFTERNOON AN ELEPHANT BELLOWS IN THE DOCK-yard. The same unmistakable sound I heard as a girl when the Ringling Brothers Circus came to town. When I ask the long-shoremen about the cries, they scoff and point to the tires rubbing against the pier. But the bellowing just gets louder, more plaintive. Long-necked cranes, gliding on rails, form a colony of giants as they build the hives of the city. Robert Bly, disappearing into de-mentia, would have led us to the elephant, guided our hands along her girth, taught us how to read the news of the universe in her wrinkled hide. He who knew so well that the hymn of the melancholic brims with the tears of things.

I'M THREE, SHE SAID, HOLDING UP FOUR FINGERS. HER grandfather fed her almonds from his pocket. Her pink raincoat was covered in winged horses so he told her about Pegasus. Being a northern girl, she asked, *Was he made of snow?* Which reminded him of sluicing steel runners on the wooden sleigh and reins draped loosely in his own grandfather's hands. Talking to her was like riding a merry-go-round. Painted horses plunging through white drifts. Him going up just as she was coming down.

FROM TIME TO TIME, THE MOON GETS TIRED OF BEING THE moon. It hides in the bowl of blood oranges on the counter. At breakfast, the mother cuts, peels and gives each child a quarter section. She knows there is no way to avoid the tumult. Sirens break the silence of the sleepy town. She knows that on the quarter moon when one boy is trampled by a wild horse, another digs a new well. Still another child wakes and listens as her brother slips into the moonless night. Closing the door quietly, he leaves home to strike out on a new and brave adventure.

EVERY WORD HE WROTE FLEW OFF THE PAGE. SOME WERE observed swooping above the Catedral de Santa María de la Sede one Friday shortly after midnight. Lovers milled about the fountain and somewhere, in the shadows, an amateur was playing a Spanish guitar. Nobody knew the war had ended. Searchlights continued to scan the skies. When the old air raid siren in the park went off, every poem, every story, every sentence he'd ever written rose in one panicked movement. A sight he tried, and failed, for the rest of his life, to describe.

A FIVE-YEAR-OLD ASKS HIS MOTHER IF THE CLOUDS ARE solid and wants to know why, when he looks up, he can't see the old people and their old cats. I must have dozed off. The trees were bare when I fell asleep but now their leaves are that impossible newly minted green. Tom Waits is bellowing downstairs and any second now someone I love is going to walk through the door. I want to know why the clouds told the Serbian poet their names in the quiet of a summer afternoon. And why didn't he share those names with the rest of us? Perhaps they did not translate into English. Perhaps the old want to stay hidden and keep their secrets all to themselves.

IN OUR BASEMENT, THE WRINGER-WASHER BARKED LIKE a baby seal. Strangers showed up with offerings of raw fish wrapped in newspaper. My mother thanked them and started giving weekly reports on the pup's progress. Brigitte Bardot sent a handwritten note on perfumed stationery applauding the rescue effort and chiding Sophia Loren for wearing fur. In the end, it got out of hand and my mother told the strangers, who had become her dearest friends, she had released the seal into the ocean. *Look*, she said, pointing to a bald head bobbing in the gray waves, *he looks just like Gandhiji without his glasses on.*

ALL MORNING WIND HAS BANKED A GREY WING OVER THE city. On the prairies it is a cry in a stairwell, a foundling. On the coast, a sail of salt. An ancient highway between Hakuba and Otari. As much as anything, we want to know that when the boat capsizes we can hang on. We will not necessarily understand. Take Nijinsky's last journal entry for instance: *My little girl singing ah ah ah...she wants to say everything is not horror, but joy*. When you died, wind shook the windows. You, who conjured Charlemagne, left us here unarmed and wildly unprepared.

PROMETHEUS IS AT IT AGAIN. HIS BEDROOM DOOR IS LOCKED but the smell of sulphur is unmistakable. The thief of fire has succumbed to pyromania. In Bruges, there's a sculpture of him driving a carriage drawn by Pegasus. You can find it in a small square in Walplein on a narrow cobblestone street filled with cafés and bars. He's easily distracted by all the good cheer. Last winter he forgot to light a fire and his hands turned blue with cold. But really, he's a loner. In his room, he's building something out of matchsticks for the science fair. The little charred heads like so many hooded executioners.

SINCE THE STROKE, I HAVE FORGOTTEN WHAT IT IS I NEED to practice. Every morning I sit at my desk like an eager pupil awaiting instruction. I snap at my husband as the hours pass and nobody comes to write on the chalkboard. In the studio, ballerinas in pink satin slippers balance on trembling legs. All the best images are on the cutting room floor and, like a fool, I keep trying to piece them together. Nothing kept the poet from playing left-handed pieces with his one good arm. On the streets of Västerås, in December, a passerby was sure to hear Haydn through the crack of an open window.

AFTER THE FLOOD, CREATION STORIES FLEW OFF THE shelves. *How do we begin again*? The people asked. Frantic booksellers ordered whatever they could get their hands on — origin stories, cosmogonical myths, Anishinaabe legends, Romanian folktales and Yiddish fables. Mud oozed in the streets and sucked the shoes off an old man who had ventured out to find milk for his cat. People took sides. Historians spoke of a land bridge while Indigenous elders whispered of a time before humans when the ancestors were feathered and scaled. *What do you mean we emerged from a gigantic clamshell?* I grilled my husband. Unfazed, he screwed the sun back into its socket and pulled the beaded metal chain — flooding our room and all the surrounding lands with light.

MY NEIGHBOUR IS A MAGICIAN. YESTERDAY HE CLAPPED his hands and my yard filled with owls. At first I thought it was snowing but it was only white feathers falling from the sky. My mother's illusions were of another kind. Like certain poems, hers changed my life. One Christmas, she conjured four Trinidadian sailors on our doorstep. They played steel drums all day while a suckling pig roasted on a spit in the kitchen. Another time, she answered the phone and turned the house into a room of grief. My neighbour says Houdini was his grandfather. I believe him, he has not learned to lie. One of the owls had a woman's face. It was familiar but I can't quite place it. These are my thoughts but not my words.

PART TWO

(after the photographs of Diane Arbus)

Nothing is ever the same as they said it was —
It's what I've never seen before that I recognize.

— Arbus

Five members of the Monster Fan Club, N.Y.C. 1961

THE MEMBERS OF THE MONSTER CLUB ARE MEETING again. They gather after school to practice being the scary people they think they are. Little boys who you might not otherwise notice — jean cuffs rolled up, arms draped casually over each other's shoulders. The Cyclops sits beside a pigeon-toed beast with missing teeth and ears shrivelled like melted plastic. The ghoul wears shorts, his bony knees scraped from falling off his bike. The fanged demon with warts on his nose has one foot tucked awkwardly behind the other. His shoelace is coming undone and there's a black hole where his eye should be. And you pity them. Not the boys, but the monsters. The horrible monsters who don't wish to frighten us, but for whom there is no choice.

Child with a toy hand grenade in Central Park, N.Y.C. 1962

THE BOY IN THE PHOTO HAS INFILTRATED MY DREAMS.
He interrogates me all night without words. We are two mutes
with different music in our brains. In the dappled light, he
looks like a bird that's fallen out of its nest. A fledgling. His left
hand's hooked and clawed, his right holds a plastic grenade
from the Army Surplus store. He's pinned to the past in a kind
of murderous taxidermy. A little blonde Bavarian not from
Bavaria. Head tilted slightly as if hearing green notes, songs,
calls. So strange and lonely he makes my teeth hurt.

Kid in a hooded jacket aiming a gun, N.Y.C. 1957

HIS MOTHER DRESSED HIM FOR THE COMING STORM regardless of the weather. Fed him lasagna and black cherry soda, pinched his pudgy cheeks and stroked his saw-tooth bangs. Killer in a bunting bag. White leather holster cinched over his coat, he took aim. It was his job to look after her. You're the man of the house now, they told him. He slept with the gun under his pillowcase. Elvis sang *Peace in the Valley*. The night was a black sea. *And the beasts from the wild will be lit by a child.* For now, the wolf at the door tamed, the bear at the window gentled.

A Jewish giant at home with his parents, in the Bronx, N.Y. 1970

LIKE ANY GIANT, HE HAD A CHILDHOOD. TEL AVIV, CROWDS, an empty phone booth ringing on Salameh Street near the Old Jaffa market. The notches on the doorjamb ceased when he turned twelve. There are only so many things giants can do. Some cross river valleys in long strides leaving small lakes in their wake. Others become wrestlers and spend their lives pinning angels to the mat. Look at him, hunched over in his parents' living room. He's trying not to intimidate, but he can't help it, he feels like a cat that's cornered two terrified mice. Eddie's still growing into himself. You can see it in his eyes.

The Junior Interstate Ballroom Dance Champions,
Yonkers, N.Y. 1963

NOBODY PREPARED THEM FOR *AFTERWARDS*. POOR darlings. Nobody told them that posing in the empty gym would be awkward like waking in a stranger's bed. They offer themselves with gravity — the young straining to be adults — their party clothes a little ridiculous in the morning light. You can see, in the dress her mother hemmed for future competitions, how thrift can look like poverty. It's clear, observing him grasshopper-legged in his white dinner jacket, that he believes he's the old moon holding the new moon in his arms. The piano lid is closed, the bench empty. Still she hears it — one quiet note played for a secret eavesdropper.

Identical twins, Roselle, New Jersey, 1967

UNCANNY SISTERS OF THE MANSION. WHAT NEWS DO YOU bring? Is there snow in heaven? What work is in your hands? Have you come to sweep the gravestones here on earth? When the lights faltered, and the hallways darkened, people came out of their rooms holding candles. Their faces lit like lanterns floating into the night sky. The ghosts too numerous to count. You are twinned like snowflakes cut and pasted on a class-room window. Here and not here at the same time. A collector's dream. If one is good two must be better thinks the lepidopter-ist hunched over the magnifying glass in his cluttered room.

The Backwards Man in his hotel room, N.Y.C. 1961

A STORM IS BLOWING IN FROM PARADISE. BENJAMIN'S angel of History has returned to a seedy room wearing a see-through raincoat. Face turned toward the past, feet toward the future. I thought his outstretched wings would fill the room; instead they hang limply down his back. *The angel would like to stay, awaken the dead, make whole what has been smashed* but he's booked at a children's birthday party after which it's all-you-can-eat Wednesday at the food court. Coming and going at the same moment, he practices for hours a day, searching the past for a way forward. Little things: disappointments, reprimands, jobs lost here and there, sleepless nights where, even in dreams, he does not triumph. All these, like a pile of debris, have grown skyward in front of him. *Angelus Novus*, when disillusioned, he loops himself into a human pretzel and basks in the applause.

Windblown headline on a dark pavement, N.Y.C. 1956

WIND THUMBS THROUGH THE NEWS. THE PAGE RADIANT
for a moment like a planet wheeling through darkness. *What is
unclear to us now will be revealed at the end of time,* wrote the
Apostle Paul. Or not. The girl who slept in a graveyard in Eilat
kept looking for a sign. For an ancient language to be revealed
by a match in the pitch black. Hieroglyphics illuminated by the
glow of a hand-rolled joint passed in a circle. What flares
briefly catches our eye. Papers lit and falling. A cry. How do we
talk to one another from the sanctuary of our own solitudes?

Boy stepping off the curb, N.Y.C. 1957-58

NO TIME TO THINK OR CLAIM MISTAKEN IDENTITY. YOU can see it in his face — not fear but surprise. A whirlwind is rushing toward him. In the hospital room, an old woman, pointing to the corner, whispers, *where have you been*? *What took you so long*? But here I go again, making notes about the three heavens — the birds, the stars and Elijah — when it's only a boy stepping off a curb. His hand emerges from his sleeve like a newborn animal. Just let him blink and carry on across the street without mishap, without a glance backwards. Ignore the tall column approaching like a waterspout. Stop pretending it could be anything other than Chekhov's black monk.

Jack Dracula at a bar, New London, Connecticut, 1961

YOU WERE A BOY OF EXCESS. IT WAS NOT ENOUGH TO BE
in the world, you wanted to be your own universe. What others
saw as freakish, you saw as text. A life's work. Your body bloomed
like a black flower in an otherwise ordinary garden. People
stared in disbelief — frightened of their own coveting desires.
Drawn to the strangeness of each petal they imagined skies with-
out stars, night without day, the squid-inked shores of Menorca,
flocks of black umbrellas. When the other kids were picking
blackberries, you emerged from the bushes stained and bleeding.
An insoluble contradiction, hidden in plain sight.

Woman carrying a child in Central Park N.Y.C. 1956

YOU'VE BEEN CARRYING THAT CHILD FOR YEARS THROUGH bombed out streets, along boulevards mad with the joy of liberation, across oceans into the green heart of a foreign city. As grave as Pietà walking through the People's Garden. Yours is a fugitive beauty. Did you know that in the summer gardens of St. Petersburg, a policeman watches every leaf to catch it before it touches the ground? Dead weight in your arms, he's so much heavier now than when you started out. Winter is approaching, soon your fingerless gloves — lovely as they are — will be of no use. Before there were public parks, people picnicked in cemeteries, spreading their blankets between gravestones. The War ended long ago but here you are, just now, walking toward us. How will you know it's over? How in god's name will you ever set him down?

Girl with a pointy hood and white schoolbag at the curb,
N.Y.C. 1957

THE GRIMM BROTHERS ARE SIPPING SCHNAPPS AT THE
Caffe Dante in Greenwich Village. Jacob is sketching out an-
other fairy tale. The main characters are a girl with a pointy
hood, a wolf and an old woman. Wilhelm is searching for a
flat to lease. He's done with morals and teachable moments
about the safe world of the village and the dangers of the for-
est. High on the balustrades, flying monkeys and griffins keep
watch over the streets. There's always a dark shape lurking in
the background. A looming storm, perhaps. A shadow stooping
over the city. Standing at the curb, you look a bit like a garden
gnome. It's not your fault; your grandmother still dresses you
for the old country.

PART THREE

for Albert Ezra Levy

...a custodian of griefs and wonders.
— Seamus Heaney

BEAR WITH ME. I'M TRYING TO SUMMON UP MY FATHER as a whale. There are peoples more adept at this than I am. The Makah, the Nootka, the old whalers of Nantucket. He looks like Lear now — at least the way I imagine the old king. Wispy white hair and sunken cheeks, teeth yellowed like ivory. His eyes, when he opens them, look upon lands he has never seen before. His body fills the canvas sling perfectly. There are holes for his fins and a fine sheen clings to his leathered skin. He lies still as he's moved through the air from bed to chair. Trusting, the way an animal trusts a human to deliver it back to its wild and familiar home.

RIDING HOME IN THE AMBULANCE, I TUCKED MY KNEES in tight so as not to bump the stretcher. I was studying your face. Memorizing it. Out the back window, the golden California hills receded. We swayed as if we were in a fishing boat headed to open water. When the paramedic asked, *Who's the sitting President*? you roared back to life, spitting and sputtering. Your old warring self. At Vineyard Road, the back doors opened and you were held for a brief moment between earth and sky; before the wheels hit the ground and off you went, a casualty on an improvised litter, into your own grievously listing house.

AT NINETY-ONE, YOUR FEARS ARE THOSE OF A BOY — THE dark closet, the bully on the playground, a headless horseman galloping toward you through the trees. Your hands curl on top of the covers as if holding on tight to the monkey bars, swinging your legs above the dirt, unable to release your white-knuckled grip for fear of falling into the abyss. When I attempt to straighten your fingers, you resist and, rung by rung, climb back up to where you are unreachable.

HE'LL JUST SLIP AWAY, THE NURSE SAID. AND ALL I COULD think of was a boy's mad scramble up an impossible slope. Pebbles rolling like ball bearings underfoot. She meant, I'm sure, that you'd slip out the door, unnoticed, like a sober guest when the party gets going. But all I could see was you losing your footing. Scree piled around your hospital bed, rock shards glinting at the base of the cliff. The whole mountainside unstable. On a piece of torn paper, tucked inside a book on the bedside table, a hastily written note said, *Something that was secret will emerge and something that was known will retreat into secrecy*.

YOUR LUNGS — THOSE LITTLE SACS YOU'VE CARRIED LIKE a goatherd across the desert — are filling up. You're becoming floodplain, sediment: habitat to great blue heron, osprey and otter. With each breath the tide sweeps in altering the shoreline. Water pours into the moat around the crumbling castle. Bishop's bird, obsessed, runs erratic across the sand. Just as you, obsessed, turn toward your death. When I ask where you are, you point to a dark shape disappearing into the depths and all I can think is: *Leviathan behind whose glistening wake one would think the deep had white hair.*

IN THE LIVING ROOM, THE OXYGEN TANK SNIFFS EVERY three seconds like someone with a runny nose. The neighbour's dog, *sans* voice box, wheezes like an asthmatic. Friends drop off Thai and whisper in the kitchen. It's so quiet in the world. Nothing is quite as it seems. There's an old woman pinning a pattern on a mannequin in the sewing room. She's been stitching and tearing apart the same dress for one hundred years. In bed, the fledgling opens his mouth for one more bite of lemony cake.

FLOATING ON A MAKESHIFT RAFT AT THE FAR END OF THE room you were on display. There's no getting around that. Somebody placed a three-legged stool beside your bed. Harder, more transitory than an armchair, calling for short visits only. People took turns, thinking they were comforting you when really it was the other way around. Everybody was welcome. The gardener with his grimy nails, a mislaid child, an old love. Even Jupiter's bird whose wingspan darkened the room. All were welcome. Nobody was turned away.

GATHERED AT YOUR BEDSIDE, YOUR CHILDREN MEASURED the time between breaths as if counting the interval between thunder and lightning. Three seconds saw you moving over dry grasses in the leonine hills; five through vineyards to the open sea. Seven had you at the mountains in a country you'd left behind. By ten it was clear the storm had passed to another valley. Pushing away from the table, neither full nor hungry, grateful to have shared a meal, you thanked each one of us. Who were you, I wondered? Why had we not met before? *Just as our room is now,* goes the old Hassidic tale, *so it will be in the world to come. Everything will be as it is now, just a little different.* Not for you. It was the end — the nothing to come — you welcomed. You follow me now like a common word on the tip of my tongue. The harder I try to remember, the more it evades me.

LIKE BAUDELAIRE'S MOON DESCENDING HER STAIRCASE of clouds, your youngest stretched her body over yours and pried your eye open to see where you had gone. A thin film, like pond scum, had already begun to form. Holding your eyelid up with her forefinger, she pulled down the lower lid with her thumb. And all that the moon loved — *water, clouds, silence and the night; the immense green sea* — looked back at her while the TV, set on Fox News, droned on inaudibly in front of your empty recliner.

THE HORSES, WHEN I FINALLY FIND THEM, IN THE DRY hills near the reservoir, seem to be waiting for me. They don't move or open their eyes. Like old people sleeping in the sun, they know who's come to visit and who has not. I was not allowed to wash or dress your corpse. Nor light a candle in the dark house. There was no raft pushed out to sea and nothing set on fire. The words of the mourning prayer *yitgadal v'yitkadash sh'mei raba* were indecipherable. This is what I've come to tell the horses. Their ears tilt toward me. The half-circle pencil sweep of their jawlines exactly like the ones in *The Sketchbook of Horses*. On this dusty hill, a lone vulture circling overhead, their long heads bow in consolation — for I know now, that's what this is.

Notes and Acknowledgements

Thanks to the journals in which some of these poems have appeared: *Prism International, The New Quarterly, Prairie Fire, The Malahat, The Winnipeg Review, Germination* and *subTerrain.*

Thanks to Brian Kaufman, Karen Green and Cara Lang at Anvil Press for their expertise and enthusiasm and for not having travelled too far from the passion of the early days fueled by pots of coffee, day-old baked goods and whisky.

I'd like to thank Marijke Friesen for reading the manuscript and creating the perfect cover for this book of poetry.

I am indebted to various people for their editorial advice — particularly Alayna Munce, Patricia Young and Patrick Friesen. As well, my gratitude for all members of the Ladies Fiction Club.

Thanks to Andreas Schroeder and Sharon Oddie-Brown for so generously sharing their cottage on the ocean.

Thank-you to the Canada Council.

To my siblings: Mike, Caroline and Margot. I feel so lucky to have shared our father's last days with each one of you.

And for my love, not the cook, the other one. Always. Always.

The poems in Part 2 are ekphrastic poems based on photographs by Diane Arbus. Should the reader be interested in seeing the photos, they can be found online by searching the titles.

In the poem "I try to follow your lead" ... on page 45, "Charles" refers to Charles Simic.

Eve Joseph's two books of poetry, *The Startled Heart* (Oolichan, 2004) and *The Secret Signature of Things* (Brick, 2010) were both nominated for the Dorothy Livesay Award. Her nonfiction book, *In the Slender Margin* was published by HarperCollins in 2014 and won the Hubert Evans award for nonfiction. The book was named one of the Top 100 picks of the year by the *Globe and Mail*.